The Careless Animal

The Careless Animal

Nine Ecological Detective Stories

Ada and Frank Graham, Jr.

Doubleday & Company, Inc.
Garden City, New York

Library of Congress Cataloging in Publication Data

Graham, Ada.
  The careless animal.

  SUMMARY: Discusses nine cases throughout the world where man's careless actions have had unexpected results on his environment.

  1. Human ecology—Juvenile literature. [1. Human ecology. 2. Ecology] I. Graham, Frank, 1925– joint author. II. Title.
GF48.G72   1975   301.31
ISBN 0-385-00603-9 Trade
ISBN 0-385-01828-2 Prebound
Library of Congress Catalog Card Number 73-14222

Preface

The puffin is sometimes called the clown of the world of birds. Its enormous triangular red bill reminds people of the false nose worn by a clown in the circus. Otherwise, the puffin is a small black-and-white bird which spends most of its life at sea, diving for fish. When it comes to the surface it often carries five or six of them, drooping like silvery mustaches from the sides of its wonderful bill.

At one time the puffin found protection in the vast reaches of the sea. But recently some puffins were found dead in the English Channel. Scientists examined their bodies. In the puffins' stomachs they found long, narrow plastic strips.

The investigators were puzzled. What were the plastic strips? How did they get into the English Channel and then into the puffins' stomachs? The scientists decided to do some detective work.

A puffin with a bill full of sand eels. (*Eric Hosking from National Audubon Society*)

They learned that the plastic strips came from a German factory that made corsets. The factory dumped its waste plastic into the Rhine River. The river's flow carried the plastic strips into the North Sea. From there, the tides and currents carried the strips into the English Channel. Puffins mistook them for the slender little fish on which they feed, and swallowed them.

When the managers of that German corset factory dumped their waste plastic into the Rhine River, they weren't thinking about puffins, or about any other living things that their plastic strips might harm. They simply thought about the wastes they had to get rid of. The Rhine seemed to be the most convenient place to dump them.

But did the plastic strips kill the puffins? No one knows for sure. There is so much else that is harmful in the sea today that some other substance might have killed these birds.

The sea has always helped to bring our world closer together. Throughout recorded history man has set out on voyages of discovery or trade. But today the sea helps to carry our mistakes around the world as easily as it once carried ships bearing gold, spices, and livestock. A country that makes a great technological mistake sends it from its shores just as it once might have exported tea or grain. The winds, tides, and currents will make certain of that.

Oil should be a true benefit to all mankind. But through his careless ways, man has let oil escape from his tankers, refineries, and offshore oil wells. The ocean currents spread the oil to places far from where it escaped. There it does damage not suspected by the people whose carelessness let it flow into the oceans. Oil ruins beaches. It kills valuable shellfish. It coats the plumage of thousands of beautiful sea birds and eventually poisons them.

No part of the ocean escapes. In the book, *The Ra Expeditions*, Thor Heyerdahl, the famous explorer, described his trip across the Atlantic Ocean on a raft. In the middle of the ocean, hundreds of miles from any land, he and his crew tried to wash their shirts in sea water. It was no use. Floating gobs of oil made the water too dirty!

Man uses DDT and other long-lasting pesticides to kill insects on his farms. But these poisons drain from the land and finally find their way into rivers, lakes, and oceans. There they enter the bodies of small sea animals. Many of these animals die. Others are eaten by large fish and birds, which, in their turn, are poisoned.

This book tells the story of how many of man's actions have had surprising effects on the world around him. In a few cases these surprises have been pleasant ones. But in most cases they have been unpleasant, doing harm to man or to the creatures with which he shares this planet.

An unusual kind of pollution—soot on the water from Jacksonville, Florida's electric generating station. (*Wide World Photos*)

The stories in this book take you around the world to show that people of many different countries too often forget that everything in this world is somehow connected. We are all a part of the same great framework of nature. We may solve all of the engineering problems in building a huge dam, or in harnessing the power of the atom. But we will let ourselves in for a nasty surprise if we forget how complicated nature really is.

Scientists who study complicated relationships in nature are called ecologists. They examine the connections between one part of the natural world and another. They often are able to see how changes in one part of our environment can have an effect on another part of our environment many miles away. They often are able to see that when one kind of animal is put in danger, other creatures—including man—may be put in danger too.

Scientists—or ecologists—stepped in to solve some of the problems created by thoughtless people who did not ask enough questions. But even while you are reading this book, other unthinking people are creating new problems for all of us. Man hasn't yet learned from the mistakes of the past.

Acknowledgments

This book could not have been written if it were not for the dedicated work of many scientists in different parts of the world. These men and women discovered the clues and pieced them together to show how carelessly planned projects came to have dangerous effects on man or his fellow creatures. They deserve our gratitude.

In particular, the authors are grateful for special help given by Chaplin B. Barnes of the National Audubon Society; William H. Drury, Jr., of the Massachusetts Audubon Society; William A. Dunson of the Pennsylvania State University; Giora Ilani of the Israel Nature Reserves Authority; and William A. Newman of the Scripps Institution of Oceanography.

During our research we found the following books helpful as sources:

The Careless Technology, edited by M. Taghi Farvar and John P. Milton (Doubleday & Company, Inc., Garden City, New York, 1972).

ACKNOWLEDGMENTS

The Last of the Ruling Reptiles, by Wilfred T. Neill (Columbia University Press, New York, 1971).

Science and Survival, by Barry Commoner (Viking Press, New York, 1967).

In their research the authors also depended on articles appearing in the following publications: *Audubon, Medical World News, Natural History,* the New York *Times,* and *Science.*

The authors are also grateful to the staff of the Bangor Public Library for their gracious help.

ADA AND FRANK GRAHAM, JR.
Milbridge, Maine

Contents

The Careless Animal

CHAPTER ONE

The Mystery of the Bolivian Cats

The people in the town of San Joaquin in Bolivia's highlands were puzzled. Not long before, every house had its share of cats. The cats were valued by the people because they killed the mice and other small rodents which came into the town from the surrounding countryside. Now the cats themselves were dying.

It was all very strange. No one had seen anything quite like it before. First, the cats began to shake all over. Then they grew listless and stopped eating. After a few days they died. The people had no idea why so many animals were dying from this new "cat disease."

Widespread illness, of course, was not new to the people of Bolivia. This large country in South America—it is about

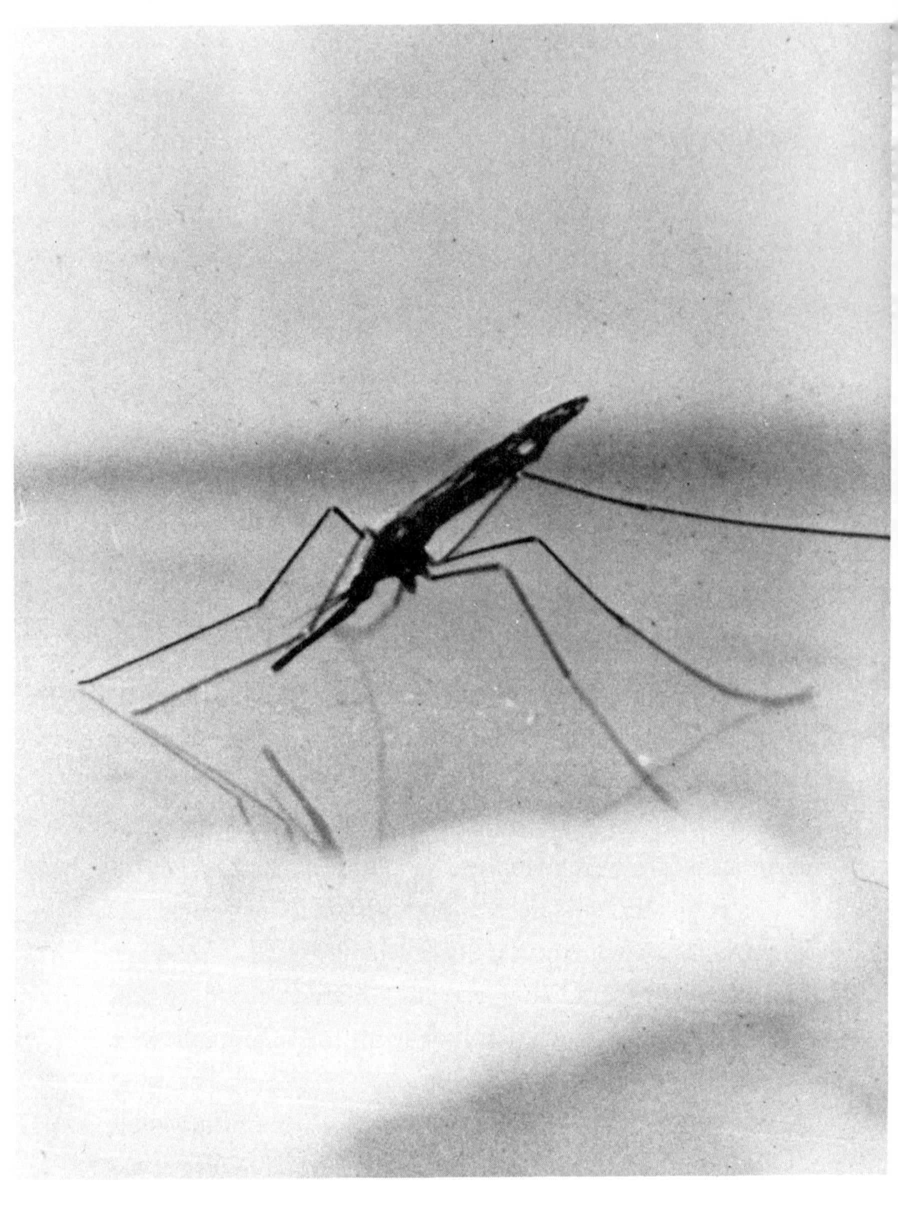

The *Anopheles* mosquito. It may be a carrier of malaria. (*Center for Disease Control*)

the size of California and Texas combined—is thinly settled. It has no seacoast of its own. Like most other tropical countries, Bolivia is troubled by serious insect pests. These pests help to spread diseases such as malaria among the people.

After World War II the people of Bolivia and of many other countries around the world believed that their pest-insect problems were solved. European chemists had developed a marvelous new insecticide which they called DDT. It was the most effective chemical man had ever used to kill insects.

Soon, wherever there was an insect problem, DDT was used. Low-flying planes sprayed large quantities of DDT on farms where insects ate the crops, and on forests where other insects damaged the trees. It was spread over marshes where mosquitoes bred.

For a while DDT seemed to be a complete blessing for man. But DDT is a long-lasting poison. It does not go away. It remains in the environment for long periods of time and kills other living things as well as insects. In many cases DDT killed large numbers of birds and fish. It also killed beneficial insects which eat the harmful ones.

DDT has even more harmful effects, scientists learned. It causes some kinds of birds to lay eggs with thin shells. The eggs break easily and the new generation dies. DDT has also been found to cause cancer in some laboratory animals. No one knows if human beings eventually will show harmful effects from the use of DDT.

But DDT was still used regularly in towns such as San Joaquin. There was no doubt that it did a good job in killing mosquitoes. In one way, DDT was good for man because fewer mosquitoes meant fewer cases of malaria. Malaria, with its chills and fever, is a weakening disease common in tropical areas.

Several times a year an event took place in San Joaquin that might be seen in many tropical towns. Public health workers arrived to try to get rid of the mosquitoes. They went into every house with spray guns and coated the mud walls with DDT.

DDT lasted a long time on the walls. For many weeks afterward it went on killing mosquitoes. Many of the local people were too poor to buy screens for their doors and windows, so, mosquitoes flew into their homes. Usually, as they do in any home, the mosquitoes landed first on the walls. In San Joaquin the walls were soaked with DDT. Before they had a chance to bite the residents and infect them with malaria, the mosquitoes died.

But strange things began to happen in San Joaquin. The cats kept dying. Children, playing in their homes or in the streets, often saw small, mouselike animals called *lauchas*.

Spraying a mud hut with DDT. (*Center for Disease Control*)

These animals appeared in larger numbers than anyone had ever seen before. What were they to think?

Then a great tragedy struck the town. People became ill. Many of them died. The local doctors knew that the people were suffering from black typhus. This is a dangerous disease which is caused by a virus, and it killed more than three hundred people in San Joaquin.

Although the local doctors knew what the disease was, they did not know how it came to San Joaquin, and they needed help in controlling it. The United States Government organized a team of doctors. The team was led by Dr. Karl M. Johnson of the National Institute of Allergy and Infectious Diseases.

Dr. Johnson and his team flew to Bolivia. They came to help the local doctors, of course, but they also came to do some detective work. They wanted to find out why black typhus had struck this town in such a remote part of the world. If they found the answers to their questions, they might prevent the disease from striking there again.

In the doctors' books, black typhus was also called by the longer name of Bolivian hemorrhagic fever. The doctors knew that the virus was spread among human beings by other living things, just as malaria is spread by mosquitoes. A creature which spreads a disease is called a vector. The search began for the black typhus vector.

Dr. Johnson and his team collected mosquitoes from the

town and examined them. None of the mosquitoes carried traces of the virus. The first investigation had gone nowhere.

Then they collected other small organisms in the area, such as mites and ticks. They found that none of these carried black typhus, either. The list of suspects was growing shorter.

While the doctors carried on their investigation, they also asked questions of the townspeople. Both the adults and the children remembered seeing large numbers of the little lauchas. Just before the black typhus struck, the lauchas were all over town. They were seen wherever food was stored and around the town's water supply.

Could the lauchas be the vectors that the doctors were looking for? The stories the townspeople told gave a clue. The doctors set out traps and poison. When they had collected a number of lauchas, the doctors examined them and found the black typhus virus.

There was one more point of proof. After all of the lauchas had been trapped or poisoned, black typhus disappeared from San Joaquin.

But the case was not yet completely solved. Why had these wild rodents suddenly appeared everywhere in San Joaquin? Again, the townspeople gave Dr. Johnson and his team a clue. The people spoke of the strange "disease" that had killed their cats.

Had the cats died of black typhus too? Dr. Johnson did not think so. The cats had started to die long before black typhus appeared among the people of San Joaquin. Dr. Johnson took some cats and injected them with black typhus virus. The cats remained healthy. This experiment proved that black typhus does not affect cats.

So far the doctors had been unraveling the mystery through hard detective work. They had worked late into the night examining all kinds of organisms for traces of the disease. They had spent many hours asking questions of the townspeople. Then they had a stroke of good luck.

They learned that when the San Joaquin cats had died of the strange "disease," a local doctor put several of their bodies in a deep freezer. Now Dr. Johnson was able to prove a theory he had started to piece together.

"The cats' symptoms had seemed odd," he said. "The cats would have the shakes, get sick, linger on a few days, and die. It looked to us like DDT poisoning."

The doctors took one of the frozen cats from the freezer. They packed it carefully in ice and shipped it by air to an expert on DDT at the U. S. Public Health Service laboratory in Atlanta, Georgia. Soon a report came back. Dr. Johnson's theory had been proved. There was enough DDT in the cat's brain to lead the expert to believe it had died from DDT poisoning.

Now Dr. Johnson was able to put together piece by piece the full story of San Joaquin's tragedy. The cats had once helped to keep the lauchas from coming out of the forest and living in town in very large numbers. Then the public health workers had sprayed the walls of the houses with DDT. The cats had rubbed their bodies against the walls and picked up DDT on their fur.

Cats are always licking their fur. When the San Joaquin cats licked their fur, they swallowed the long-lasting poison, DDT, and died.

After all the cats were dead there was nothing to keep the lauchas out of San Joaquin. They invaded the town by the hundreds, living near human food and water. Because these little animals carried the black typhus virus, they spread it through San Joaquin's food and water supplies. Soon the people became ill and died.

The chemists who made DDT were concerned about one thing. They wanted to make a poison that killed insects. In this they did their job well. But these chemists forgot that everything in this world is connected. The poison that kills mosquitoes kills other creatures too. By solving one problem, man sometimes sets in motion complicated events that bring new problems of which he has never dreamed.

CHAPTER TWO

Barramundi

In the rivers of northern Australia lives a large fish called the barramundi. It is a favorite of sport fishermen. It puts up a lively fight on the line when hooked, and its flesh is tasty. Yet a series of wars on the other side of the world seriously reduced the numbers of the barramundi in Australian waters.

This story concerns crocodiles and soldiers. Crocodiles have a bad reputation, but in many cases this is unfair. In this case the villains are not the crocodiles but the soldiers.

Crocodiles and their close relations, alligators, are the living descendants of the dinosaurs and other great reptiles which ruled the earth ages ago. They live only in warm, wet places.

Crocodiles are well provided by nature with the means for protecting themselves. Only the most powerful creature would risk being caught in the grip of the crocodile's crunching jaws. And the crocodile itself is protected by the tough armor of its hide.

But the crocodile's mighty jaws are no match for a man who stands out of its reach with a high-powered rifle in his hands. And the crocodile's tough hide, rather than protecting it, is more likely to be the reason it is hunted and killed by men.

The hides of crocodiles and alligators are now extremely valuable. They are used in making shoes, belts, wallets, and handbags. Shoppers pay high prices for them in fashionable stores.

All over the world crocodiles and alligators are being destroyed for their hides. Some kinds of crocodiles are nearly extinct. In the southern United States, alligators were wiped out in many areas.

In Florida's Everglades the destruction of the alligators caused trouble for other living things too. Water is hard to find in parts of the Everglades during the dry season of the year. But the alligators deepen and enlarge water holes with their bodies. Fish, birds, and other wildlife gather at these "gator holes." The alligators eat some of them, of course. But the rest of the animals have the water they need to get through the dry season.

When the alligators were killed, there were few water holes for the other creatures in the Everglades. Laws were passed protecting the alligators. But the hunters came in at night. The price of hides was so high that the hunters risked arrest to kill alligators.

Finally more laws were passed. It became a crime for stores to sell the hides of alligators that had been killed illegally in the United States. But the hides of crocodiles killed in other countries—where they are not protected—could still be sold.

One of the places where crocodiles were killed for their hides was in tropical Africa. Africa is not really a continent of steamy jungles and crocodile-filled streams as many people imagine it to be. Much of it is desert, grasslands, and open woodlands.

Most of the crocodiles in the Nile, Africa's great river, had been killed many years ago. But in Central and West Africa there are jungles where several kinds of crocodiles live in the streams and rivers.

The crocodiles were hunted ruthlessly in those places. Their hides were shipped to markets in Europe and America. But during the 1960s, civil wars broke out in the Congo and, later, in Nigeria. Trade and shipping stopped in those war-torn countries. There was no way to get the crocodile hides to the markets.

The demand for hides was still high. In times of shortage, prices rise. Crocodile hides had to be found somewhere. The prices paid for crocodile skins in Australia went up, and more people began to hunt them.

The easiest to hunt were the fresh-water crocodiles. These crocodiles are neither large nor dangerous, most of them being under six feet long. They live in the smaller rivers and creeks. Australian aborigines, the true native people, often bathe close to them in the forest streams.

Soon the fresh-water crocodiles became very scarce. Most of them had been killed for their hides. The hunters then began to turn their attention to the large salt-water crocodiles.

The salt-water crocodiles are widely scattered across Southeast Asia, the East Indies, and northern Australia. They are able to swim long distances in the ocean. One of them swam to the Cocos Islands, which are six hundred miles from any other land.

Salt-water crocodiles grow very large. Some may reach twenty feet in length. They are also very dangerous. Most crocodiles do not attack human beings, but these large salt-water crocodiles have often attacked and killed people in the water. Witnesses have described how they grabbed swimmers by the leg, whirled them around several times, and then dragged them under to their death.

In Australia, the salt-water crocodile is often found some

Skinning a crocodile in North Queensland, Australia. (*Australian News and Information Bureau*)

distance up the larger rivers and streams. People have seen them leap out of the water to seize their food. But for the most part they live on fish, frogs, turtles, and other living things in the water. The hunters began to shoot them everywhere in northern Australia for their hides.

"Five years ago on any river in the Northern Territory you might see fifteen or twenty crocodiles in a single day," an Australian scientist told a reporter. "Now you may see none in weeks. Then people realized that the population of the fish we call barramundi seemed to be going down at the same time the crocodiles were disappearing."

The sport fishermen complained that there were few of their favorite fish, the barramundi, to catch any more. Scientists began to wonder if there was a connection between the disappearance of the barramundi and the salt-water crocodile.

Then the scientists remembered what had happened in Egypt. Some years before, the crocodiles in the Nile had been slaughtered for their hides too. The Nile crocodiles used to feed on a number of fishes that ate the Nile perch. When the crocodile disappeared, these other fishes greatly increased their numbers. They ate most of the perch in the Nile.

Australian scientists began to look more closely at the life history of the barramundi. The barramundi also is a member of the perch family. When it is small it is often eaten by the salmon catfish. But crocodiles eat a great many salmon catfish.

The scientists then realized why the barramundi was disappearing from Australian rivers. As one of the scientists said, "When there are fewer crocodiles to eat salmon catfish, naturally there are more salmon catfish to eat the barramundi."

The wars of Africa had been felt in the rivers half a world away.

CHAPTER THREE

The High Dam at Aswan

A great dam has risen on the Nile River in Egypt. It is three miles long and 350 feet high. It is seventeen times the size of the famous pyramid of Cheops at Giza, which is included among the Seven Wonders of the Ancient World.

At the same time that this dam was being built, an Egyptian fishing fleet appeared in the Atlantic Ocean. It was the first fishing fleet sent into the Atlantic by any Middle Eastern country.

What was the connection between the two events? This is the story of the Aswan High Dam and the effect it has had on people and their ways of life—even those who live many hundreds of miles from where the dam was built.

Egypt lies in a part of the world that until very recently had changed little since the time of the Old Testament. But modern engineering skills are causing Egypt to catch up in development with the rest of the world. Great building projects are being planned and carried out. But sometimes these projects have effects someplace else which their creators never expected.

Egypt takes its life from the Nile. Much of Egypt, which lies in the northeast corner of Africa, is a vast desert where man can find neither water nor food. So most of Egypt's people live along the Nile.

The Nile rises in Ethiopia and Central Africa. Every spring, ever since recorded history began, the river has rushed northward into Egypt, swollen by the spring rains. Its fresh water carries with it the rich earth it has washed from the land along the way.

In Egypt the river overflows its banks. It leaves behind it a rich layer of earth and minerals. Only in these fertile strips that the Nile has created along its banks, and at its mouth, can the Egyptians farm their land. The regions of Egypt that the Nile doesn't touch remain barren deserts.

The Nile rushes on through Egypt to the Mediterranean Sea. Before the high dam was built at Aswan, between 50 and 100 million tons of soil were carried every year past Cairo in the river's flow. As the river enters the sea, it drops more of its load of earth and minerals.

The Nile has created a special world there too. This is the delta, which is new land built up by the Nile at its mouth. The new land is very fertile.

But the Nile does not exhaust itself even then. When it flows out into the Mediterranean Sea it is still a source of life. Its gift to the Mediterranean is the great quantity of fresh water it carries in its spring floods.

The Mediterranean Sea depends on a flow of fresh water. Although this sea is composed of salt water, it differs from the great oceans. It is surrounded by land. It lies in a warm climate.

The hot sun beats down on the Mediterranean. A great deal of its water is evaporated at a time when little rain falls into it. But the amount of salt always remains the same. The Mediterranean, in many places, becomes too salty even for fish to survive.

But fish have always found it easy to live in the eastern Mediterranean. There, the Nile carried into the sea its fresh water and its nourishing minerals. These elements mixed with the salt water to form a good breeding ground for fish.

The Egyptian people need fish. Egypt raises very few beef animals because the country has many diseases that affect animals. So fishing became an important Egyptian industry in the eastern Mediterranean Sea. Fish, especially sardines, were found in all the local markets.

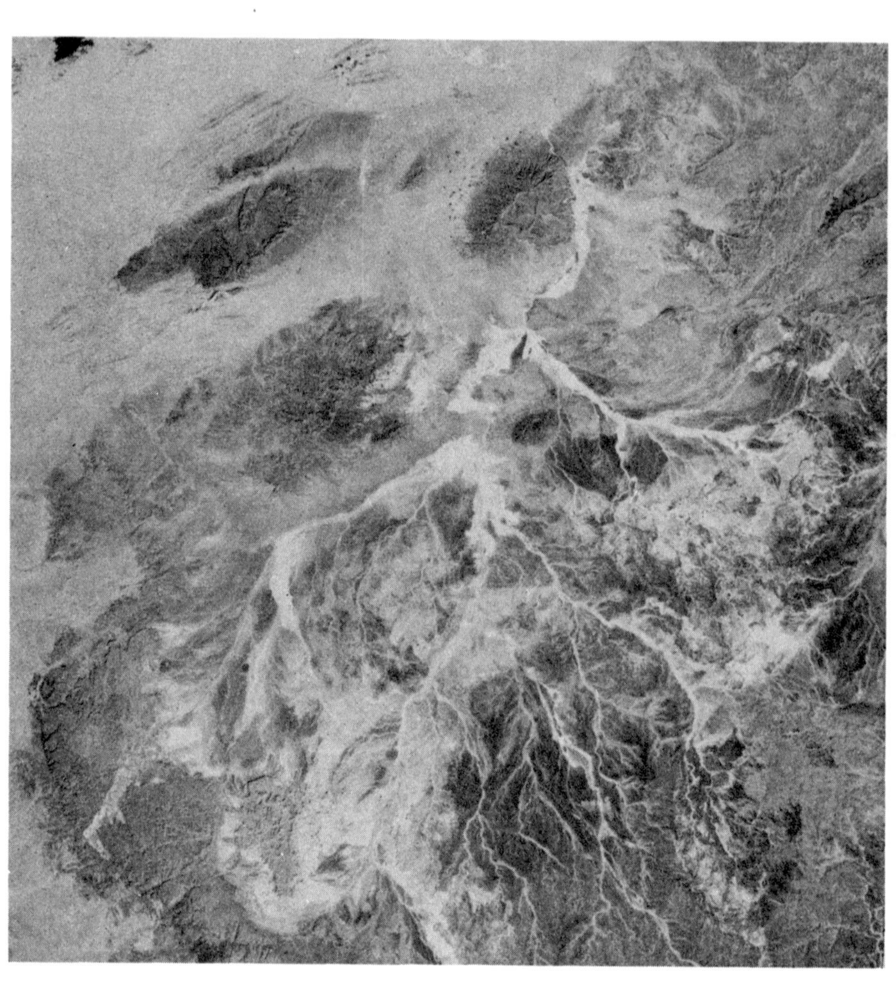

A satellite photograph of the Nile Valley. (ESSA)

No wonder the Nile was sometimes compared to a god! It fertilized and watered the land, which would have been barren without it. It created the fertile delta. And it enriched the eastern Mediterranean Sea from which the Egyptians took their fish.

Still, Egypt was a poor country. Most of the land was desert where crops would not grow. Great numbers of people were crowded onto the rich land of the Nile Valley and the delta. The land in those areas was fruitful, but there was a limit to the number of people it could feed.

So once more the people of Egypt turned to the great river. In 1902 they built a granite dam on the river near the city of Aswan. At that time it was the largest dam in the world. It measured one and a quarter miles long and 176 feet high.

The dam was built chiefly to control the river. It held back some of the Nile's rushing waters in the spring. In this way not all of the river's water flowed into the sea at once. Some water was held back to irrigate the fields in time of dry weather.

But by 1960 Egypt wanted to develop more industry. It needed a great new source of power. Its government decided to build a new dam on the Nile which would supply water power for industry. The dam would be more than twice as large as the old one at Aswan.

The Russians provided the money for Egypt to build its new dam. They also sent engineers and technicians to teach the Egyptian people the most modern ways of constructing it.

A great new dam rose in the desert near the old one at Aswan. Built of earth and rock fill, it was a marvelous feat of engineering. A scientist who has been there described the new dam:

"Hundreds of thousands of boulders well over two yards thick litter the faces of the dam like small pebbles," the scientist wrote. "For thousands of acres, as far as one can see, the land is littered with storage yards and sheds, repair centers, roadways, and power transmission lines."

The huge pile of rock and earth blocked the greatest river in the world. The water spread out behind the dam, covering the desert, as well as some valuable ancient ruins. It formed a lake almost three hundred feet deep, three hundred miles long, and about six miles wide.

The Egyptian people were proud of their new dam. They had built well, working with the advice of good engineers. But now they are beginning to realize they could have used the advice of some good ecologists too.

The Aswan High Dam, as they call it, will change the lives of the Egyptian people in more ways than they had

The Aswan High Dam under construction. (*Novosti from Sovfoto*)

expected. The water power generated at the dam will provide electricity for their homes and factories. In this way it may improve the living conditions for millions of people.

But the dam has its unexpected effects too. It has cut down the flow of the Nile. The floodwaters no longer rush downstream as they did before, carrying rich earth and minerals to be dropped in the delta. Some scientists are afraid that if the delta is not continuously built up each year by the Nile, the Mediterranean Sea will sweep back over it. Then Egyptian farms and the lakes of the delta with their valuable fish will be lost.

The Aswan High Dam has also reduced the flow of fresh water into the Mediterranean Sea. The water near the mouth of the Nile has become very salty again. The fish have almost disappeared.

In 1962 Egyptian fishermen caught more than 18,000 tons of sardines in the eastern Mediterranean. Three years later they caught only five hundred tons of sardines.

"I searched the fish markets of the delta coast," a scientist said. "I found not a single sardine at a time of the year when they used to be abundant."

What had happened to the sardines? They could no longer live in the salty water off the coast of Egypt. The huge schools of sardines had moved farther east along the coast in search of fresh water—into the part of the Mediterranean Sea that is controlled by Israel.

The strange series of events that occurred in Egypt will happen more often in other parts of the world. The engineers and the ecologists did not come together and exchange information before the dam was started. This marvelous engineering feat did what it was supposed to do. It controlled the waters of the greatest river in the world. But it had effects that no one knew anything about before the dam was built.

And that was why, after the dam had been built and the sardines had disappeared from the nearby coast, a fleet of new fishing boats made its way out of an Egyptian port. These boats were built with money provided by the Russians. The boats were worked by crews trained by the Russians. They did not stop at the Egyptians' old fishing grounds in the Mediterranean Sea. They went on westward through the Straits of Gibraltar into the Atlantic Ocean.

It was a long way to go, but at least the Egyptians knew they would be able to find fish.

CHAPTER FOUR

The World of the Eskimo

The scientists of the United States Atomic Energy Commission had thought of a wonderful plan. At least, many people thought it was wonderful. They called it "Project Chariot."

It seemed very simple. A new deep harbor was wanted on the northwest shore of Alaska. People had been talking about the need to put nuclear energy to work for the good of mankind. So the scientists thought it would be a fine idea to blast open a new harbor by using hydrogen bombs. The project would save money and a lot of work.

The scientists knew that such a project could not be carried out everywhere. It would be too dangerous if people lived close by. But there in northwest Alaska the nearest

Eskimo villages were many miles away. No one would be hurt by the hydrogen blasts.

The Atomic Energy Commission went ahead with its plans for Project Chariot. But there were scientists in the United States who were not so sure that Project Chariot was really such a fine idea after all. Had the Atomic Energy Commission made a thorough study of what all of the project's effects might be?

The Atomic Energy Commission's scientists knew just how powerful their hydrogen bombs were. They knew that they could blast a hole deep enough in Alaska's shoreline to make a fine new harbor for large ships. They also knew their hydrogen bombs were not powerful enough to blow up people who lived many miles away.

But nuclear weapons also give off harmful radiation. Radiation is made up of high-energy rays which are very similar to X rays. These rays can cause sickness or death in human beings. When a nuclear bomb explodes, the dirt and other particles which are sucked into the fireball become coated with radiation. When these particles finally fall back to earth, scientists describe them as "fallout."

The Atomic Energy Commission said that not much radiation would fall on Alaska. Most of it, they said, would drift high into the sky and be blown away. Only a little of it would fall on the Eskimo villages. It would not be enough to hurt the people who lived there.

But these government scientists should not have been so certain. Nuclear weapons such as hydrogen bombs are the most terrible weapons man has ever invented. There was already some evidence about how terrible they could be.

During World War II, the United States dropped the world's first atomic bombs. Thousands of people in two Japanese cities were killed or badly wounded. Other thousands of Japanese people escaped the explosions, but they sickened and died later on from the effects of radiation.

After the war, an even more powerful nuclear weapon was invented. It was called the hydrogen bomb. But many people said some good might come from these terrible weapons. They said that nuclear energy could be made to perform useful tasks for man.

The United States, Russia, and other countries went on testing their hydrogen bombs. Scientists who were in charge of these tests said that no harm would come from them because they were made in remote places. The radioactive particles, they assured the public, would drift up into the atmosphere. They would be blown by winds around the world. No single group of people seemed likely to get a large dose of radiation.

The Atomic Energy Commission went on preparing for Project Chariot. In the United States, meanwhile, the scientists who weren't so sure about Project Chariot's safety

A thermonuclear detonation in the Pacific—February 1954. (*Look-out Mountain Air Force Station*)

went on with their work too. Some of them formed the Committee for Nuclear Information. They called the group CNI for short.

The CNI scientists made studies of their own. They carefully searched through the reports of other nuclear scientists all over the world. They began to see that the fallout from nuclear explosions was more serious than anyone had realized.

Some studies showed that nuclear fallout was dropping onto pastures where cows grazed. When the cows ate the grass, radioactive particles ended up in their milk. When children drank this milk the radioactive particles entered their bodies. Some of the children who drank the radioactive milk later developed nodules, or small tumors.

The scientists also learned that nuclear fallout is not spread evenly around the world, as the Atomic Energy Commission thought. Winds carried most of this fallout to the Northern Hemisphere.

The new information contained another alarming fact. Eskimos in the Arctic had been examined to see if they had traces of radioactive fallout in their bodies. Scientists did not believe they would find much radiation in Eskimos. But they were wrong—Eskimos carried more radiation in their bodies than any other group of people in the world!

How could this happen? How could Eskimos, who live

Caribou. (*Leonard Lee Rue III*)

in the remote Arctic, be exposed to more nuclear fallout than other people? The men of the Atomic Energy Commission did not know.

It took scientists who knew something about the Arctic region to solve the problem. The answer involves the ancient way of life of the Eskimos, as well as that of a large grazing animal called the caribou.

Eskimos live in the land of ice and snow. They reached America thousands of years ago from Asia, crossing the narrow strip of water into what is now Alaska. Unlike the American Indians, who lived in the forests and prairies farther south, the Eskimos settled above the treeline. There the weather is too cold and the summers are too short for the larger trees and plants to grow. Vegetables cannot be grown in most of that region either. So Eskimos eat mostly fish and meat.

A favorite food of many of the Eskimos is caribou meat. Caribou are wild reindeer. Their broad hoofs allow these large animals to travel great distances over the Arctic's bogs and snow.

It is hard to imagine how the barren land of the Arctic is able to support many thousands of large grazing animals such as the caribou. The secret of the caribou's ability to live in the Arctic is that they eat tiny plants called lichens.

Lichens are really two plants in one. They consist of an alga and a fungus living together. Lichens have no roots. The alga absorbs water from the air and makes food by photosynthesis. The fungus gives the plant its shape and keeps it from drying out. So these two plants work together to form a single plant that is able to live in very severe climates.

Lichens support caribou in the Arctic, where it is often difficult to find other food. Over great areas of land, lichens are almost the only plants caribou can find to carry them through the severe seasons.

But, because lichens take their water directly from the air instead of from the soil, they absorb large amounts of nuclear fallout from the sky. Other plants take up much of their minerals through their roots and so some of the radioactive particles are strained out before they enter the plant tissues.

The caribou, feeding mostly on lichens, built up large amounts of radiation in their bodies. Eskimos in many parts of the Arctic live mostly on caribou meat. They, too, built up large amounts of radiation in their bodies. Because of their special diet, they were soon exposed to more radioactive particles than any other group of people in the world.

This was the story that the CNI scientists were able to

Reindeer lichen. (*Frank Graham, Jr.*)

tell the public. They asked the Atomic Energy Commission to cancel their Project Chariot. Fallout from the explosion of the hydrogen bomb, they pointed out, would cover wide areas of land where the Eskimos hunted for food.

At first the Atomic Energy Commission did not want to call off Project Chariot. The Commission had already spent many millions of dollars preparing to blast open the new harbor. Even the Eskimos had not complained about the coming explosion. No one had ever told them that they were already carrying dangerous amounts of radiation in their bodies.

The scientists of CNI and many other people wanted to get the story to the Eskimos themselves. But few Eskimos read newspapers or listened to the radio in their remote villages. There was another way to get the story to them, however. Most Eskimo villages have tape recorders. The CNI scientists wrote bulletins about radioactive fallout, put them on tape, and sent bulletins and tapes to some Eskimos in Alaska. The news spread quickly.

"The tape recorder is one of the greatest inventions as far as the Eskimo is concerned," a biologist in Alaska said. "Every village has several tape recorders. There is a constant traffic in tapes from one village to another. The information about Project Chariot got into the tapes and it literally swept the Arctic coast, from Kakhtovik all the way down to Nome and below. I recall, also, meeting an Eskimo driving a dog team on the trail one time and, by golly, he had a copy of the CNI Bulletin tucked inside his parka!"

Now the Eskimos knew all about the danger they faced. Project Chariot was called off. Several years later the United States and Russia signed a treaty in which they agreed not to test nuclear weapons in the open environment.

These governments had made wonderful plans for using nuclear weapons as tools. The invention of these weapons was a remarkable scientific victory. But the nuclear scientists had forgotten to include in their studies the world of the Eskimo, the caribou, and the little plants called lichens.

The scientists who discovered that part of the story won a great scientific victory too.

CHAPTER FIVE

Hurricane Agnes

Early on a summer evening a man and a woman were driving along a road on the coast of eastern Maine. They saw a thirteen-year-old boy whom they knew walking by the side of the road. They stopped to offer him a ride.

"Hop in, Fred," the man said, opening the door for him. "Where are you going?"

Fred climbed into the back seat. He was polished and scrubbed, looking as if he had just stepped out of a bathtub, and he wore a new jacket.

"I'm going to the movies in town," he said.

"You look very prosperous," the woman said, smiling.

She was accustomed to seeing Fred around town, wearing old work clothes and boots, and spattered with mud.

Like many of the other boys in this coastal town, Fred earned some money by digging clams when he was not in school. It was hard work, combing back the mud with short-handled rakes at low tide.

"I feel rich," Fred said with a proud look on his face. "I made fifty-six dollars digging clams today!"

Fred and every other man and boy who dug clams on the coast of Maine were making money that summer of 1972. Fred guessed he was making two and a half times as much money as he would have made only a year earlier. It was not that he was working any harder. A disaster had occurred seven hundred miles to the south that brought good fortune to the people of this Maine town.

The car stopped in front of the movie theater.

"Good luck with your digging tomorrow," the woman said as Fred got out.

"Thank you," the boy said. "I'd better make the money now, because the price won't stay high forever."

Fred was right. As long as human beings have lived along that coast they have harvested clams and other shellfish. The heaps of shells left behind in kitchen middens by the Indians tell the story of how they prized clams as food. The earliest European settlers dug clams in New England's tidal bays. But no one before had ever been so richly rewarded for digging clams as Fred and the other clam diggers were that summer.

The soft-shell clam is a very sensitive creature. Although it is found on both coasts of the United States, it lives in the largest numbers on the coasts of Maine and Massachusetts and in Chesapeake Bay, south of Washington, D.C. The water in which it lives must be salty.

A young soft-shell clam is tinier than a grain of sand. It spends the early weeks of its life floating on the water's surface. As its shell grows, the clam settles to the bottom of the bay. There it makes a burrow in the mud. Its long "neck" reaches out of the burrow to strain food from the water which moves back over it with every new tide.

The soft-shell clam's food is the microscopic collection of creatures called plankton. To get enough plankton to eat, the clam must pass a great deal of water through its body. If this water contains even tiny amounts of chemicals or other man-made poisons, the clam may die.

Until recent years, America's chief source of soft-shell clams as food was the tidal coast of New England. The clams are easy to dig there. Twice each day the tides uncover the large bays, leaving the mudflats bare. The clam burrows appear as small round holes in the mud. Anyone who is digging clams knows he will find one several inches deep at the bottom of this small hole.

In Maine, people make money digging clams. Not much equipment is needed. Before Fred goes clam digging, he pulls a pair of hip boots over his old pants. When the tide

Digging clams with a clam hoe. (*Susie Fitzhugh*)

goes out, he picks up his clam hoe and a clam roller and walks out onto the mudflats.

His clam hoe isn't really a hoe at all. It looks more like a four-pronged pitchfork, with a short handle joined to the prongs at a sharp angle. His clam roller is a wooden box which has a handle running across its top. The slats in the sides and bottom of the roller are spaced to let water run in and out of it easily. When he wants to wash the mud from the clams, he simply dips the roller in water. This washes the clams.

Fred needs sturdy boots when he walks out into the mud. The mud is soft and he sinks in it to his shins. Like all good clam diggers, Fred has learned to walk easily through deep mud.

When he is on the mudflats, Fred looks for the small holes that dot the mud and tell him where he will find clams. Then he sinks his hoe into the mud, combing it back with one hand while picking out the clams with the other. He tosses the clams into the roller. A lot of clams are wasted by this sort of digging, of course. The prongs on the hoe crush many of the clams when the digger pushes it into the mud.

A clam roller holds a half bushel of clams. When Fred fills up one roller, he puts it aside and begins to fill another. When the tide rolls back over the mudflats, Fred and his friends take the rollers to shore.

A clam being drawn from the mud. (*Susie Fitzhugh*)

Clams are an important part of Maine's economy. Fred sells his clams to a dealer, who distributes them to markets and restaurants. They may be sold in the shell, to be eaten as steamed clams, or taken out of the shell and eaten as fried clams or put in chowder. When Fred started digging clams, he was paid $2.50 by the dealer for a roller, or $5.00 for a bushel.

Soft-shell clams also grow in great numbers in Chesapeake Bay, but they are not so easy to harvest. This huge bay—it is two hundred miles long—is bordered by Virginia and Maryland. Some of America's most famous rivers, including the Potomac, the James, and the Susquehanna, flow into the bay.

But tides do not empty the Chesapeake, as they do many of Maine's bays and coves. Most of the Chesapeake clams burrow into mud that is always covered by water. They cannot be dug with hoes if they are under several feet of water.

Chesapeake clams became "big business" only in recent years. Hydraulic dredges were designed to harvest the clams. These dredges are long arms fastened to the sides of boats. They dig into the mud under the water, scooping up clams. Large numbers of clams may be harvested cheaply in this way in a short time. In many markets, Chesapeake clams took the place of the Maine clams that are dug more slowly with hoes.

In late June 1972, one of the worst tropical storms in history roared up the East Coast of the United States. Hurricane Agnes, as it was called, brought the high winds that are part of every big storm. It also brought torrents of rain.

For days the rain poured down on the Middle Atlantic states. Roads and railways were washed out, farmland was ruined, and homes were swept away.

Hurricane Agnes badly battered the Chesapeake Bay region. The Susquehanna River—the largest river flowing into the bay—overflowed in the most destructive flood in 183 years. All of the rivers poured a wild tangle of uprooted trees, broken telephone poles, and smashed liquid-gas containers into the bay.

The rains continued. Every river, stream, and gully carried its load of wreckage into Chesapeake Bay. Of course, the trees and telephone poles and the floating remains of houses were easy to see. But the rampaging flood carried other things into the bay, too. It was those other things that were to make known their effects even in Maine coastal towns many hundreds of miles away from the hard-hit Chesapeake region.

The floodwaters swept over farms, carrying away the dangerous pesticides that the farmers had sprayed on their fields to kill insects. The floodwaters washed over city

The results of Hurricane Agnes in Laurel, Maryland. (*United Press International Photo*)

dumps, carrying off masses of rotting garbage. The flood-waters clogged city sewers and drains, carrying away foul-smelling sewage before it could be treated at the city's sewage plants. All of this was added to the water in the bay.

Chesapeake Bay suddenly became an enormous cesspool. In its waters mingled sewage, garbage, and dangerous chemicals. The wastes of modern civilization had been swept from man's control by a tremendous storm.

The danger of disease lay in the Chesapeake's murky water. Soft-shell clams, by their nature, are sensitive to pollution. As they take in water when they are straining their food from it, their soft bodies absorb the poisons that are in the water.

The public health authorities acted quickly. No clams were allowed to be taken from the polluted water. The clam boats of Chesapeake Bay, their dredges idle, remained tied to their docks.

But people still wanted to eat clams. The fish markets and the restaurants turned to other sources. In Maine, the dealers bought all the clams they could get. The prices rose to $8.00 a bushel . . . $10 a bushel . . . $12 a bushel . . . and even $14 a bushel!

For a few weeks, at least, Maine clams once more were the leaders on the market. Boys such as Fred, with their fathers and their brothers, pulled on their hip boots and trooped out onto the mudflats. Hurricane Agnes, for some people in Maine, meant only showers and thick fogs. But for Fred and the other clam diggers, the hurricane brought the best-paying days of their lives.

For their extra money, they had to thank a polluted bay seven hundred miles to the south.

CHAPTER SIX

The Flamingos of Sinai

War broke out between Israel and Egypt in early June, 1967. It was a lightning war. Israeli planes knocked out the Egyptian air force and their ground defenses. Israeli tanks rolled across the sands of the Sinai Desert, smashing the Egyptian Army.

The war lasted only six days. Israel had won. Its troops held almost all of the Sinai peninsula, which was the eastern part of Egypt and covered an area of land larger than Israel itself.

This war, though so brief, was like all wars. Death and destruction were left in its path. Strangely, "the Six-Day War" proved to be a benefit for one special group of creatures—the flamingos of Sinai.

Israeli troops in the "Six-Day War." (*Wide World Photos*)

The flamingo is one of the world's most beautiful birds. Much of its plumage is pink. In flight, a flamingo looks like a large pink cross in the sky—with its great wingspread, its long neck thrust out before it, and its long legs trailing behind. It honks like a goose.

The flamingo comes from a very old order of birds. There were flamingos on earth while the great reptiles still ruled the land and before most of the mightiest mountain ranges we know today came into being. The flamingo probably is more closely related to storks than to any other group of birds.

No other bird has such a long neck and long legs in proportion to its body. Nor does any other bird, or any other animal with a backbone, imitate the flamingo's custom of eating with its head upside down while its body is right side up!

The flamingo usually feeds where the water is at least a little bit salty. When it feeds, it turns its head upside down so that the top of its bill rests against the muddy bottom of the pool. Then it works its lower bill up and down. This action pumps the mud and water through slits in the top of its bill. Its tongue has tiny structures on its edges which strain the small animals and plants it eats from the liquid.

There are several different kinds of flamingos. They nest

Thousands of flamingos at their breeding grounds. (*Mark Boulton from National Audubon Society*)

in the West Indies, South America, southern Europe, Asia, and Africa. Some kinds are colored pink only on their wings. Other kinds are colored a bright pink over most of their bodies.

There are no colonies of wild flamingos in the United States. The most famous collection in this country is the group of captive flamingos at Hialeah Race Track in Florida. Every once in a while a flamingo escapes from the race track. Someone sees it in the Everglades and thinks that that is where it has always lived.

For a long time a few flamingos nested on the Sinai peninsula near the Suez Canal. The Sinai touches the Mediterranean Sea in the north. To the south, much of it is desert or granite ridges. Many people believe that it was on Mount Sinai in the southern part of the peninsula that Moses received the Ten Commandments. (Other people say this occurred on a different mountain nearby.)

The salt marshes in northern Sinai make good feeding places for flamingos. Some flamingos tried to stay all year long and nest there. But Arab fishermen often pulled their boats into the marshes during the nesting season. They would take the flamingos' eggs and young for food.

In 1967, when the war broke out, there were only a few flamingos in the Sinai's lakes and marshes. For a few days the Sinai Desert was the scene of great battles. Then the war stopped.

Israel and Egypt were still enemies, and they went on with their dispute—this time with words—about the Sinai peninsula. Only Israeli soldiers were allowed to go into the region. Everyone else, including the Arab fishermen, was told to keep out.

The next year some Israeli scientists were permitted to go into the Sinai. They saw about a thousand flamingos in the salt marshes. In 1972 Giora Ilani, a young Israeli biologist, was sent into the Sinai to study the wildlife there.

Ilani looked at the salt marshes through his high-powered binoculars. What he saw amazed him. A huge pink haze seemed to spread out across the marshes. The haze seemed to quiver in the sun.

"But that whole expanse of pink was really thousands and thousands of flamingos," he later told a reporter from the New York *Times.* "Only early and late in the day, when the sun is low, can the eye pick out the individual shapes of birds."

Ilani kept on watching the flamingos. He estimated that there were 11,000 flamingos in the marshes. Many of these birds were nesting, and he could see young birds everywhere.

This large colony of flamingos had come to the Sinai because of the war. When the Arab fishermen were not allowed into the area, there was no one to bother the birds. They were able to nest and raise their young in peace—in the marshes where plenty of food was available to them. The only one watching them was Giora Ilani, the Israeli biologist.

From that time on he followed the lives of these colorful birds. He learned much that has been of interest to scientists all over the world. In 1973 he counted 19,600 flamingos in the two areas where they lived.

One area was a swamp called A-Tina, which lies at the edge of the Suez Canal. The water in this swamp is so salty that fish do not live in it. There is a kind of small shrimp, however, that lives in A-Tina. This shrimp is a favorite food of the flamingo.

Giora Ilani counted 11,000 flamingos in this swamp alone. Many of them live there all year round, feeding in the winter and staying to nest in the summer.

The other place where flamingos live is not far away. It is a large lagoon lying along the Mediterranean coast of the Sinai peninsula, and it is called Bardawil Lake. It is larger than the A-Tina swamp, but not as many of the flamingos live there. Ilani counted 8,600 of them. He found that the water in Bardawil Lake is not as salty as that in the A-Tina swamp. There are many fish in the lake, mostly mullet, but it does not have the little salt shrimp that the flamingos seem to like best.

Not many of the flamingos stay at Bardawil Lake during the summer. They fly to other places. Ilani doesn't know where they go to nest, but it is a good thing for the flamingos that they do leave. Bardawil Lake is not in the military zone. Anyone may enter it. If the flamingos stayed there to nest, the Arab fishermen would come from the nearby villages to take their eggs and their young.

What will happen to the flamingos of Sinai?

"The future of the birds depends, in my opinion, on the political situation," Ilani says. "If the A-Tina swamp stays in a military zone, then nobody will be able to bother the birds. But if real peace is made between Israel and Egypt, then the fishermen will come back and the birds cannot nest there."

Giora Ilani hopes that men will be able to solve their differences and live in peace. But he also hopes that they will be able to find a way to keep that beautiful pink haze over the marshes of Sinai.

CHAPTER SEVEN

Gulls, Gulls, and More Gulls

The U. S. Air Force pilot was taking off. His F-101B fighter plane roared down the rain-swept runway at nearly ninety miles an hour.

Suddenly there was a deafening explosion. A ball of flame shot out of the left engine. The right tire blew out as the pilot fought to bring the plane under control on the slippery runway. The plane finally slid to a stop and the pilot raced to safety just before flames destroyed the plane.

The cause of this frightening accident is now a common one all over the world. As the plane roared down the runway it struck a bird. The powerful jet engine sucked in the bird, cutting off the 'ne's power. If the plane had

An F-101B. (U. S. Air Force Photo)

hit the bird after it had lifted off the ground, the plane might have crashed.

Many people have been killed in recent years when their planes hit birds near airports. Planes have suffered millions of dollars' worth of damage. In one recent year, 566 civilian planes and more than 1,000 U. S. Air Force planes collided with birds in flight. The birds most often hit are gulls.

At first the people who managed the airports thought the problem could be solved easily. Why not simply shoot the gulls who are seen around airports? But shooting the gulls did not work. If some were shot, other gulls flew in from the surrounding area to take their place. There were too many gulls to try to kill all of them.

Why do planes hit gulls so often near airports? This is what people in the Air Force and in the airline industry wanted to know. Was it something about the planes that attracted gulls to them? Or was there a connection between the airport accidents and something else that had happened outside the airports themselves?

Gulls are among the most beautiful birds that inhabit the shorelines of the Northern Hemisphere. Both scientists and poets have marveled at the skill and grace of their flight.

There are many different species of "sea gulls." Some,

like the laughing gull—which is named for its cackling cry—have black heads. Other gulls are mostly gray and white. They are useful birds too. They are scavengers, eating garbage and refuse of all kinds, and have helped to keep beaches and other shorelines clean. Because they ate up the hordes of crickets that threatened to destroy the Mormons' first harvest in Utah, gulls played an important role in the history of that religious group.

We see gulls often today. But one hundred years ago gulls were not common along most parts of our shorelines. Hunters killed them by the thousands so that their plumage could be used to decorate women's hats. When gulls nested on the islands, people came there and gathered up all their eggs for food. Some biologists thought that gulls might disappear completely from our shores.

Then laws were passed to protect gulls and other kinds of birds. Some kinds of birds never fully recovered from the widespread shooting during the last part of the nineteenth century. But gulls, especially the herring gull of the North Atlantic, had a population explosion of their own. Their numbers grew so rapidly that in some areas they came to be looked on as pests almost as disagreeable as mosquitoes.

One such place where the gulls became pests was around the large international airport at Boston. Planes often struck gulls and other birds near Logan Airport. Sixty-two people were killed when an Electra jet hit a flock of starlings and crashed there a few years ago. Several other planes had scary collisions with gulls.

The people who ran the airlines became worried. On almost any day they could see hundreds of gulls flying over Logan. They could see gulls—large white birds with gray wings—standing in groups in the middle of busy aircraft runways. They knew these birds might cause other accidents. They still weren't sure why so many of them gathered at the airport.

When we want to know something about a subject, we ask an expert in that subject. This is what the airlines' officials did. They took their problem to Dr. William H. Drury and his fellow biologists at the Massachusetts Audubon Society.

Gulls were no strangers to the biologists at the Massachusetts Audubon Society. The Society itself had been organized in 1896 to protect gulls and other birds. And the Society's members had been watching gulls during the years of their recovery.

These biologists had seen the gulls' numbers double every twelve or fifteen years. For a long time they had been asking themselves why this spectacular increase had occurred among the gulls and not among the other birds that they were trying to protect.

Bill Drury and his assistants were given money by the United States Government to make a thorough study of the gulls and the problems they caused. They watched the gulls at Logan and the other nearby airports. They followed their movements to and from the airport every day. They made notes on the numbers of gulls, how many were adult birds and how many were young ones, and at what times of the day and the year the gulls were most numerous.

Drury and his assistants soon began to see some patterns in the gulls' behavior. There was not enough natural food around the shore of Boston Harbor to feed so many thousands of gulls. But the gulls knew where to get help from man himself.

Man, by his careless habits, had provided food for thousands of gulls in the area near the airport. At piers where fishing boats docked, the waste parts of fish littered the ground and the water. At hog farms outside the city, huge heaps of garbage were left about in the open for the hogs to eat. The largest of all the gulls' feeding places were the city dumps where trucks carried tons of garbage every day.

It was easy for Bill Drury and his assistants to follow

Gulls and our garbage. (*Ray Hunold from National Audubon Society*)

the gulls' travels. In the mornings the gulls flew to where they were able to find food. Thousands of gulls gathered around fish piers and on the roofs of fish canneries. The birds patiently waited for the fishermen to throw away the leftover parts of the fish. Squawking loudly, the hungry gulls fought each other for the scraps of fish.

Other gulls flocked to the hog farms. The scraps set out by the farmers for the hogs to eat were left uncovered. The sharp-eyed gulls were able to see the scraps from long distances away.

Closer to the city, other gulls watched carefully for the heavy trucks which carried garbage to the open dumps. When the trucks left, the gulls gathered in large groups, announcing with sharp screams their excitement at finding another day's feast set out before them.

By the end of the morning, the gulls had eaten all they wanted. Then they looked around for a flat open area near water where they could spend the rest of the day bathing and resting. Drury traced the gulls' line of flight. In many cases it led straight from the fish piers, hog farms, and city dumps to Logan Airport.

"If the people who built Logan Airport had decided to make a nice resting place for gulls right from the start, they couldn't have done a better job than this," Bill Drury said.

The gulls were satisfied at Logan Airport because it was

built near three large city dumps where they could easily get all they wanted to eat. The airport even had a dump of its own. Small ponds and salt marshes were left at the airport's edges, making fine loafing places for the gulls. Gulls, like people, spend part of their time just loafing. At night they found places to sleep on the long aircraft runways that stretched out into the darkness. Logan Airport was, Bill Drury saw clearly, the perfect place for gulls to spend their time.

During the winter, Drury and his assistants counted 110,000 herring gulls along the New England shore. More than 80,000 of these gulls lived around the large coastal cities where dumps and fish waste were always available to them. There were four times as many gulls around garbage-filled Boston Harbor as there were on the vast but less populated shores of Cape Cod. No wonder people are conscious of the gulls that seem to be everywhere about the large coastal cities!

Only once did the numbers of gulls drop sharply in the area around Logan Airport. One winter day a small child was run down by one of the big trucks that carry garbage to the city dumps. The mothers of the other children who lived near the dump were very angry. They wanted more traffic lights and other safety measures installed in their part of the city.

The mothers blocked the streets so that the dump

trucks could not pass until the streets were made safer for their children. The trucks weren't able to bring the city's garbage to the dump. This gave Bill Drury a chance to confirm his beliefs about the gull problem.

There was no longer a screaming flock of gulls fighting for food at the dump. There was nothing for them to eat there. They had to fly to other places along the coast to look for food. When that happened there were no longer so many gulls at Logan Airport. Only after the mothers settled their differences with the city, and the trucks got through to the dump, did the gulls return to the dump—and the airport.

Now it became clear why there were so many gulls at Logan. In fact, at airports all around the country the same thing was taking place. Airports and dumps are usually found close together on the edges of cities. Gulls find it easy to fly back and forth from one to the other.

The airports do not stand all alone in their communities. Biologists such as Bill Drury began to point out that gulls are not ordinarily pests. They are turned into pests by man's careless habits. When food is made easy for gulls to find, naturally they will flock to it in great numbers.

The pilot, as he roars his plane down the runway to take off, suddenly sees a large flock of birds rise up, flapping, in front of him. There is the sudden danger of a crash. The pilot had thought of himself as being alone, encased in the metal world of his plane. Now, through the carelessness of other men, a flock of wildly flapping birds were entering the pilot's world too. Man and gull were both part of one world.

CHAPTER EIGHT

Traveling Sea Snakes

The shallow water of the Pacific Ocean off the Central American beach was green and cloudy. A little farther offshore the deeper water was blue and clear. At the point where the different colored waters met, a strip of foam drifted on the waves.

Many objects collected in this foamy strip, brought together by the sea's currents. There was a clump of stringy seaweed. There was the trunk of a large tree that had been torn from land during a storm. There was a long slender "stick." A school of small fish, looking for a good place to hide from their enemies, swam just under the collection of floating objects.

Suddenly the "stick" lashed out and seized one of the

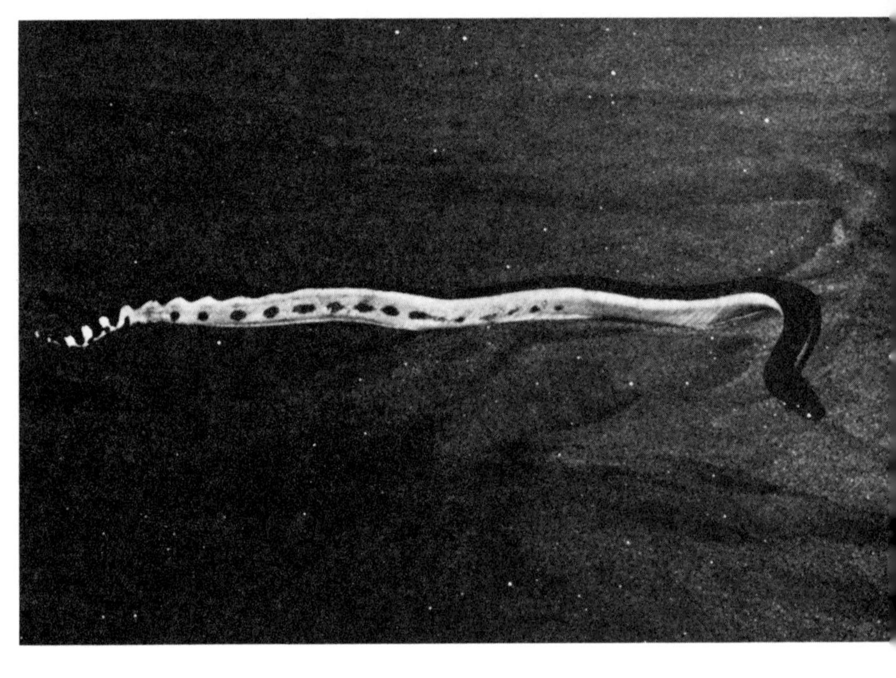

A yellow-bellied sea snake. (*Professor William A. Dunson*)

small fish. It was not a stick at all. This was the deadly yellow-bellied sea snake which had been drifting idly on the water like a stick, waiting for a fish to come near.

Sea snakes, which may grow as long as eight feet, are found widely spread through the Pacific and Indian oceans. They are related to the cobras and have poisonous fangs. Their poison is deadlier than that of any land snake. Even large fish avoid them. The unlucky fish which tries to eat a sea snake will almost surely be bitten and killed by the poison.

Until now, the Atlantic Ocean has been free of sea snakes. But man may change that very soon. Sea snakes, crown-of-thorns starfish, and other sea animals that are troublesome to man, may pass from the Pacific into the Atlantic Ocean. Here is how it may happen.

Oil companies and other large corporations find that they are able to make more money if they transport their products in very large ships. It is cheaper to carry all of a cargo of oil, minerals, machinery, and other products in one mammoth tanker or freighter than to carry it in several smaller ships.

As trade expands, the nations of the world are building more ships and larger ships. Much of this shipping passes between the Atlantic Ocean and the Pacific Ocean through the Panama Canal. But this canal, which was completed in 1914, cannot handle the great size and number of ships that want to pass from one ocean to the other today.

The men who manage some of the large corporations and the shipping lines want the United States to build a new canal. Certainly a new canal may save money for everybody eventually, and be a service to the world. But what kind of a canal should be built, and where should it be located?

The President of the United States ordered a study to be made of the possibilities for a new canal between the oceans. The people who made the study came to a decision. They said that the best place for such a canal would be through the Isthmus of Panama, close to the present Panama Canal.

But, they said, the new canal should be built in a different way. It would not be composed of a chain of locks, as the Panama Canal is. Locks are a series of basins in which ships passing through a canal are raised or lowered to the proper level.

The new canal, if it is built following the plans of the committee which made the study, will be a "sea level canal." It will not have locks. Huge gates will be closed behind the ships entering the canal so that little water will flow through. Without locks, the new canal will be able to handle more and larger ships.

According to the committee, this canal should be built in the near future. The committee report said that all the engineering problems could be solved by modern building methods. The report also said that there would be no serious scientific problems because there was little chance that sea snakes and other troublesome animals would pass through the canal from one ocean to another.

All too often in our time the world has gotten into trouble because of incomplete reports such as the one that was made for the President about the canal. For instance, the people who favored building a supersonic transport plane—an SST—said we should go ahead simply because it was possible to build one. They did not stop to think about what the plane might do to our eardrums with its sonic boom, or to our atmosphere with its harmful exhaust.

Other people said that we should use large amounts of DDT because it killed harmful insects. But they did not tell the whole story. They did not stop to think what DDT might do to other living creatures.

Our world is in trouble, then, because a small group of people plan great projects without wondering what their final effects on all of us might be. But there are scientists in America, fortunately, who are asking the question: Should a sea level canal be built between the Atlantic and the Pacific oceans? They are also asking: If it should not be built, is man wise enough *not* to build it?

These scientists know from other people's unhappy experiences that such canals can have harmful effects. Many years ago the Welland Canal was dug between Lake Erie and Lake Ontario. Sea lampreys—large, eel-like creatures—swam through the canal into the western Great Lakes. The lampreys ate so many of the white fish and lake trout that they destroyed the fishing industry there.

The Panama Canal had no such ill effects. In the middle of the canal there is a large body of fresh water called Gatun Lake. Fish and other ocean animals that try to pass through the canal will not cross this fresh-water lake. They always turn back toward the salt water of their own ocean.

There are about 8,000 different kinds of sea animals living on the Pacific side of the Isthmus of Panama. There are about 7,000 kinds living in the Caribbean Sea, which is on the Atlantic side of Panama. If a few kinds of sea animals such as the sea snake came into the Caribbean Sea, they might do great damage there.

Some people ask why sea snakes and other Pacific Ocean animals do not simply swim into the Atlantic around the tip of South America. If they do not, the reason probably is that they are tropical animals. They must live in warm water. The water close to the tip of South America is much too cold, and it would kill them.

Another committee was formed to study the idea of building a sea level canal. This committee was made up of marine scientists—men whose business it is to study the life in the ocean.

After a year of study, these scientists warned that a sea level canal might cause serious damage in the Caribbean Sea. They said that such a canal should not be built unless a good way was found to keep sea animals from passing through it. The flow of water through a sea level canal would not permit a fresh-water barrier such as Gatun Lake. Nor was it likely that engineers would be able to create a zone of water in the canal too warm for even tropical animals to enter.

The marine scientists' suggestions were not even included in the report that was sent to the President. The director of the first study accused the scientists of being "alarmists." In effect, the director said that these able scientists did not know what they were talking about.

Fortunately, the marine scientists were able to publish their findings and suggestions in other places. One scientist, William A. Newman of the Scripps Institution of Oceanography in California, reported what he had learned about the crown-of-thorns starfish.

This animal is able to live in many different places. It feeds on coral. In parts of the Pacific Ocean it has destroyed up to 90 per cent of the coral on some reefs.

A crown-of-thorns starfish. Those are coral catfish in the lower right-hand corner. (A. W. *Ambler from National Audubon Society*)

Dr. Newman showed that the starfish live on the Pacific side of the Isthmus of Panama. If a sea level canal were built, this animal would be carried in the flow of water through the canal into the Caribbean Sea. Once there, it might destroy many of the coral reefs which support whole communities of sea creatures. These coral reefs also attract many tourists to the Caribbean.

One place where there was much interest in a sea level canal was in the United States Congress. The House of Representatives asked William A. Dunson, a biologist at Pennsylvania State University, to tell its members what he thought about such a canal.

Dr. Dunson told the congressmen that diseases and parasites might be spread from one ocean to the other through a sea level canal. He also told them about his studies with sea snakes. If these animals entered the Caribbean, he said, they might destroy the food sources of many valuable fish. Also, he said, their poisonous bite has killed human beings. Sea snakes might frighten bathers away from Caribbean beaches.

"I must conclude that construction of a sea level canal would be a disaster," Dr. Dunson told the congressmen. "Let's keep the yellow-bellied sea snake in its natural place—in the Pacific Ocean."

CHAPTER NINE

One World

The month before he was killed, President John F. Kennedy spoke of his worry that man was thoughtlessly causing great damage around the world. He had come to realize that science, for the first time in history, has the power to experiment at one place and thereby cause enormous changes in many other places.

"The problem is difficult," President Kennedy said, "because it is hard to know in advance whether the effects of a particular experiment will help or harm mankind. The government has the clear responsibility to weigh the importance of wide-scale experiments against the possibility of destructive effects. The scientific community must assist the government in arriving at wise judgments."

President Kennedy was one of the first world leaders to see that our environment was in trouble. Many other people thought that all of the talk about ecology and pollution was a passing fad. They thought that these matters would soon be forgotten.

But it is likely that a turning point in the history of the world took place in 1972. By then, the leaders of most countries knew, as President Kennedy did, that each of us now shares in the mistakes of his neighbors. The actions that a country takes halfway around the world may affect each of us for good or ill.

And so the Stockholm Conference was born. In 1972 the United Nations sponsored a conference at Stockholm, Sweden. Representatives from 113 nations came together to make a start at keeping the world fit for all of us to live in.

There were differences of opinion, of course. Some countries want to move rapidly toward cleaning up the world. Other countries are willing to put up with more pollution and land destruction until they have raised the standard of living for their people.

In general, there was a split between the wealthy industrial nations and the still underdeveloped nations of the "Third World." The big industrial nations realize in many cases how they have destroyed much of their own environ-

The Stockholm Conference. (*United Nations*)

ment. Now they want to look for better ways to keep incomes at a high level, while giving people a decent world to live in.

Some of the poor countries are impatient to get their share of the world's wealth. These countries may not be as eager to listen to the advice of worried scientists about their environment. Until they, too, grow wealthy, they may go on making the same mistakes that were made in the United States, Russia, Japan, and Western Europe. They may pollute the air and water, use pesticides carelessly, and enter into poorly planned engineering projects such as dams and canals.

The results, then, will be felt beyond their own borders.

But a new spirit could be sensed at Stockholm. More than simply a flood of words came from the conference. There was a new sense of responsibility. Most nations decided to co-operate with the others.

Here are some of the things these nations have done:

People are now aware that oil or chemicals, dumped in one part of the ocean, may be carried hundreds of miles to destroy birds, shellfish, and beaches someplace else. Seventy-nine countries quickly signed a treaty promising not to dump dangerous substances in the ocean.

People are also aware that trends in fashion threaten to wipe out many of the world's interesting creatures. In the fashionable stores of Paris, Rome, and London there is a great demand for the hides of alligators, the feathers of birds, and the furs of spotted cats. This demand may push the hunted animals over the edge of extinction.

No one country can save these animals. Eighty countries have promised not to trade in the products of 375 kinds of endangered animals. They know that they must co-operate to save these creatures for everyone's enjoyment.

A few years ago there was a plan to flood the Grand Canyon behind a great dam. People now know that this foolish project would have destroyed a great national treasure which should be preserved for all the people of the world. The World Heritage Convention has been created to help individual countries preserve special areas such as the Grand Canyon. This convention recognizes the fact that such natural wonders truly belong to everyone.

These agreements among countries mean that mankind has arrived at a new knowledge of itself and the planet on which it lives. We are many different races, we speak many different languages, and we believe in many different forms of religion and politics.

But we share the same biology. Our bodies work in the same way. Our energy comes from the same sources. We are confined, at least for centuries to come, to planet Earth. We are, in a real sense, all dwellers in one world.

The symbol of the United Nations Conference. (*United Nations*)

Index

Ada and Frank Graham have written a number of books about nature and the environment for young readers. Mr. Graham, a Field Editor of *Audubon*, has traveled widely for national magazines and talked with a number of scientists about the case histories described in this book. He is the author of the highly acclaimed *Since Silent Spring* and *Where the Place Called Morning Lies*. Mrs. Graham, a teacher, has devised nature education programs and with her husband has worked extensively with children in woods, meadows, and tidal pools near their home on the coast of Maine.

Together the Grahams have written the following books for young readers: *The Great American Shopping Cart*, *Wildlife Rescue*, *Puffin Island*, *The Mystery of the Everglades*, and *Dooryard Garden*.

Ada Graham was born on a farm in Miamisburg, Ohio, and Frank Graham was born in the heart of New York City.